The Mojave Desert

By Molly Aloian

Crabtree Publishing Company

www.crabtreebooks.com

Crabtree Publishing Company

www.crabtreebooks.com

Dedicated by Molly Aloian
For Andrew Urlocker—My oasis in the desert

Author: Molly Aloian
Publishing plan research and development:
 Sean Charlebois, Reagan Miller
 Crabtree Publishing Company
Editor and indexer: Wendy Scavuzzo
Design and photo research: Katherine Berti
Project coordinator: Kathy Middleton
Print and production coordinator: Katherine Berti

Picture credits:
Shutterstock: pages 1, 4, 6, 10, 11, 12 (left and Brittlebush, Desert holly, and Ocotillo cactus), 13 (all except rattlesnake and owl), 21 (bottom), 22, 24, 25, 26, 27, 28 (bottom); Songquan Deng: page 19 (top); Jorg Hackemann: page 20 (background); Chee-Onn Leong: page 21 (top)
Thinkstock: cover, pages 8, 13 (rattlesnake and owl), 23, 25, 28 (top)
Wikimedia Commons: Alexrk2: page 5; Philip Kahn: page 7; United States Geological Survey: page 9; Stan Shebs: pages 12 (Claret cup and Mojave yucca), 14, 16 (bottom right); Cgoodwin: page 12 (Allscale); United States Navy: page 15 (top); US Library of Congress: page 15 (bottom); O'Sullivan Timothy H: page 16 (top); Edward S. Curtis: page 16 (bottom left); Eeekster Richard Ellis: page 17; Bobak Ha'Eri: pages 18 (top), 23 (top); Reno Chris: page 18 (bottom); Nick Christensen: page 19 (bottom); National Park Service: page 20 (inset)

Library and Archives Canada Cataloguing in Publication

Aloian, Molly
 The Mojave Desert / Molly Aloian.

(Deserts around the world)
Includes index.
Issued also in electronic formats.
ISBN 978-0-7787-0713-4 (bound).--ISBN 978-0-7787-0721-9 (pbk.)

 1. Mojave Desert--Juvenile literature. I. Title. II. Series:
Deserts around the world (St. Catharines, Ont.)

F868.M65A56 2012   j979.4'95   C2012-905676-6

Library of Congress Cataloging-in-Publication Data

CIP available at Library of Congress

Crabtree Publishing Company
www.crabtreebooks.com   1-800-387-7650

Printed in Canada/102012/MA20120817

Published in Canada
Crabtree Publishing
616 Welland Ave.
St. Catharines, Ontario
L2M 5V6

Published in the United States
Crabtree Publishing
PMB 59051
350 Fifth Avenue, 59th Floor
New York, New York 10118

Published in the United Kingdom
Crabtree Publishing
Maritime House
Basin Road North, Hove
BN41 1WR

Published in Australia
Crabtree Publishing
3 Charles Street
Coburg North
VIC 3058

CONTENTS

Words that are defined in the glossary are in
bold type the first time they appear in the text.

CHAPTER 1
Meet the Mojave Desert

The Mojave Desert is in the United States. It is the smallest of the four North American deserts. The Mojave spans more than 25,000 square miles (64,750 sq km) through southeastern California, southern Nevada, northwestern Arizona, and southwestern Utah. It lies between the Great Basin Desert to the north and the Sonoran Desert to the south. Long mountain ranges separated by valleys mark the transition between the hot Sonoran Desert and the cooler, higher Great Basin Desert.

Joshua Tree National Park is filled with cholla cactus and the twisted, spiky Joshua tree that grows nowhere else in the world.

Great Basin Desert

Sonoran Desert

Mojave Climate

In the Mojave, annual rainfall is from 2–6 inches (5–15 cm). During the winter months, temperatures can drop to 20°F (-7°C) in the valleys and dip to 0°F (-18°C) at higher **elevations**. In mid-May, temperatures are normally above 90°F (32°C), but will begin to climb to 100°F (38°C). Summer weather in the desert is scorching hot. Temperatures in the valleys can reach as high as 120°F (49°C) and even above 130°F (54°C) at the lowest elevations. October is one of the driest and sunniest months in the Mojave. Temperatures are often between 70°F (21°C) and 90°F (32°C).

Fast Fact

Winds in excess of 25 miles per hour (40 km/h) are not uncommon in the Mojave Desert. Some gusts reach 75 miles per hour (121 km/h)!

Plants and Animals

The most prominent plant in the Mojave Desert is the Joshua tree. This spiny-armed tree is found only in the Mojave Desert. Hundreds of other plants, such as creosote bush, allscale, desert holly, and white burrobush, also call the Mojave home. Mojave Desert animals include many kinds of insects, reptiles, birds, and mammals, but most of these animals are inactive during the hot days and **forage** only at dusk, dawn, or at night when the temperatures are cooler. All of the plants and animals in the Mojave Desert are **adapted** to the dry, harsh climate.

First Farmers

The Mojave Desert is named after a group of **indigenous**, or Native, people called the Mojave (or Mohave). The Mojave people have lived in the desert for thousands of years. They lived along the lower Colorado River in what is now Arizona, California, and Mexico. They farmed the area for hundreds of years before European explorers arrived in North America.

Hot or Cold

Most deserts are very hot places, but not all deserts are hot all of the time. Some deserts can get very cold at night and at certain times during the year. Some are even covered with ice or snow. There is little precipitation in these deserts, but the temperature is so cold that the snow does not melt. For example, the Gobi desert in China is often considered a cold desert. The Great Basin Desert is another cold desert.

Great Basin Desert

NOTABLE QUOTE

"[The Mojave Desert] is the best known, most visited, and most studied of American deserts; but it is also, in an important historical sense, the most reliably typical of American deserts, the national standard…No wonder it is the desert of definition for so many Americans— studied, loved, quarreled over."

—P. Reyner Banham, *Scenes in America Deserta*

Desert Under Threat

Today, modern civilization is a major threat to the health of the Mojave Desert. Habitat loss and pollution are threatening the desert wildlife more and more each year. One of the main reasons for habitat loss is **urbanization** from Los Angeles and Las Vegas. As the population grows in these areas, more space is needed for homes, roads, and food crops, and there is an increasing demand for **landfill** space. Habitat loss and pollution have negative impacts on the plants and animals that rely on the desert for their survival.

Fast Fact

Vast areas of the upper Mojave have been set aside for testing weapons and for **aerospace** testing. The dry desert air minimizes deterioration of the airliners.

Desert Tortoise

The desert tortoise lives in the Mojave. To escape the heat of the summer and the cold of the winter, the desert tortoise lives in a **burrow**. It has muscular front legs and long claws that are designed for digging the burrow, which is usually 3–6 feet (1–2 meters) deep. The desert tortoise spends about 95 percent of its life underground. In spring, it comes out of its burrow to eat herbs, grasses, and other plants. Most of the water the tortoise needs to survive comes from the plants it eats in the spring. It can store water in its bladder to use during the driest months. The desert tortoise is listed as a threatened species under the federal and California versions of the Endangered Species Act.

The desert tortoise has a high, dome-shaped shell that is usually brown or tan in color.

CHAPTER 2

The Mojave Up Close

A desert can be defined in different ways, but many scientists believe that a desert is any area that receives less than 10 inches (25 cm) of rain per year. Deserts lose more moisture through evaporation than they receive from precipitation. They may seem to be barren wastelands, but deserts contain a vast array of plants and animals that have adapted to the arid conditions over hundreds of millions of years.

Zabriskie Point is at the edge of the Black Mountains to the east of Death Valley. The elevated point overlooks an undulating landscape of gullies and mud hills.

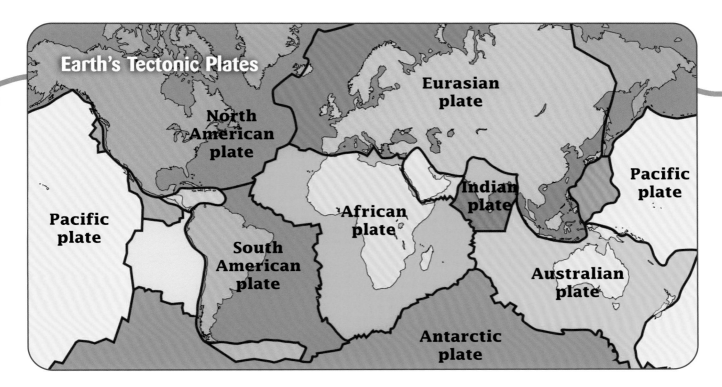

Earth's Tectonic Plates

North American plate

Eurasian plate

Pacific plate

Pacific plate

African plate

Indian plate

South American plate

Australian plate

Antarctic plate

Millions of Years Ago

The Mojave Desert formed over millions of years. In fact, during the Paleozoic Era hundreds of millions of years ago, the Mojave Desert and most of the American Southwest were covered by shallow seas. Over time, sea levels rose and fell and thousands of feet of **sediment** were deposited on the sea floors. When the shallow seas completely retreated, these layers of sediment were exposed to **erosion** from wind and water. During the Mesozoic Era, from 245–65 million years ago, Earth's **tectonic plates** collided at fault lines. Fault lines are separations or cracks in Earth's **crust**. The Pacific Plate began to slide beneath the North American plate. The edges of the plates pushed up into folds and wrinkles, creating mountains, valleys,

and volcanoes. The climate in the Mojave became even more arid than it is today, and wind and water continued to erode the land.

Mojave in the Making

Around 30 million years ago, Earth's tectonic plates began moving again and Earth's crust cracked into blocks. As the plates and blocks slid and rotated, they generated **friction** and great amounts of heat. Massive volcanic eruptions occurred forcing hot **magma** through vents in Earth's crust. Large mountain ranges formed over millions of years as the lava cooled. Evidence of past volcanic eruptions can be seen throughout the Mojave Desert. Many of these sites are part of the Mojave National Preserve, a government protected area in San Bernardino County, California.

Rain Shadow

Today, the Mojave Desert is locked deep inside the landmass between the Sierra Nevada Mountains, which are part of the Pacific Mountains System. The desert is in a rain shadow, which is a dry area of land on the leeward side of a mountainous area. Rainfall and moist air prevail on the windward side of the mountains, while arid moisture-poor air prevails on the leeward side of the mountains. This means that any moist air loses most of its precipitation before reaching the Mojave.

Fast Fact

Although the size of Earth's deserts is always changing, deserts cover five to seven percent of Earth's surface. The Atacama Desert in Chile is the driest place on Earth. Each year, it receives less than 0.01 inches (0.03 cm) of rain.

High Desert

There is a wide range of elevations in the Mojave Desert, more than in any other North American desert. Elevations range from below sea level in Death Valley to over 5,250 feet (1,600 m) on certain mountains. Most of the desert is from 2,000–4,000 feet (610–1,219 m), which is why the desert is sometimes referred to as a high desert.

The Sierra Nevada Mountains extend more than 250 miles (402 km) along the eastern edge of California, northward from the Mojave Desert to northern California and Oregon.

Dry Lakes

Dry lakes are a common feature in the Mojave landscape. A dry lake is a temporary lake. The surface of a dry lake is usually cracked and dry. But during the rainy season, it becomes wet and very soft. China Lake, Searles Dry Lake, Koehn Dry Lake, and Harper Dry Lake are four large dry lakes in the northern Mojave Desert. The National Audubon Society has named these dry lakes Important Bird Areas, or IBAs. IBAs are areas that provide important habitats for one or more bird species. IBAs include areas for breeding, wintering, and **migrating** bird species. Thousands of migrating water birds, such as the eared grebe, American white pelican, and white-faced ibis, visit these lakes in late March.

Racetrack Playa is a dry lake in Death Valley National Park. It is 3,608 feet (1,100 m) above sea level. Rocks called sailing stones move slowly in long tracks along this dry lakebed. What makes them move is still unclear.

Do Not Cross

Death Valley is a large valley near the border of the Great Basin and the Mojave. It is the lowest, hottest, and driest point in North America. Its lowest elevation is 282 feet (80 m) below sea level. Now a national park, the valley is about 140 miles (225 km) long and from 5–15 miles (8–24 km) wide. It attracts thousands of tourists and scientists each year. Settlers who were exploring the area in 1849 gave the valley its name. They endured extreme suffering while trying to cross the valley.

Close to Hollywood, many movies have been filmed in the Mesquite Flat Sand Dunes in Death Valley.

Brittlebush

Claret cup

Amazing Adaptations

There are hundreds of species of plants living in the Mojave Desert and all of them are suited to life in the desert. The brittlebush is a small shrub that usually flowers from March to June. Its leaves are covered with short hairs. The hairs act like a blanket over the leaves, **insulating** them from the hot and cold desert temperatures. The hairs also trap any moisture in the air and help prevent the plant from losing water through its leaves. Allscale, which is also called common saltbush, is another shrub found in the Mojave. To conserve water, this shrub will sometimes shed its sharp, spiny leaves. The leaves of the desert holly are gray in color instead of green. The gray color helps the plant reflect more of the hot desert sunshine. The Mojave yucca has specially shaped leaves that channel rain and **dew** to the center of the plant. The leaves also have a waxy coating that helps prevent the plant from losing precious moisture.

Allscale

Desert holly

Joshua Tree

Most people associate the Joshua tree with the Mojave Desert. It is the largest yucca in the Mojave and can grow 15–40 feet (5–12 m) tall. It has two sets of roots. One set spreads out near the surface of the ground rather than reaching far down below the ground. This adaptation allows the Joshua tree to immediately absorb any rain that falls. The other set of roots stores extra water and develops bulbs beneath the ground. Growing underground protects the bulbs from the hot and cold desert temperatures. The Joshua tree's spiny leaves are turned upward to catch any rain that falls. The plant also stores water in the stems and trunk.

Ocotillo cactus

Mojave yucca

12

Desert Design

Mojave Desert animals are also suited to life in the desert. The desert coyote has tan fur with a mixture of rusty brown and gray hairs. The different colors help the coyote hide in the underbrush and among rocks and grasses while it hunts for prey. To avoid the scorching midday heat, Mojave rattlesnakes usually hunt for rats, mice, lizards, and birds at night when the temperature is cooler. It hibernates during the cold months of late fall and winter. Banded geckos, desert iguanas, regal horned lizards, chuckwallas, kangaroo rats, burrowing owls, and bighorn sheep are other animals that live in the Mojave.

The Mojave rattlesnake has very **toxic** venom. It is one of the most dangerous poisonous snakes in the United States.

Desert bighorn sheep live in dry, desert mountains. They have large, curved horns that weigh up to 30 lbs (14 kg).

Banded gecko

Burrowing owl

Chuckwalla

Coyote

Mojave Ground Squirrel

The Mojave ground squirrel is suited to the hostile climate in the Mojave Desert. It lives mainly in the western side of the desert in underground burrows among the roots of the creosote bush. Some burrows are 20 feet (6 m) long and 3 feet (1 m) deep. The ground squirrel eats seeds, fruit, and green plants, and stores as much as possible in its burrow. It gets the water it needs to survive from the seeds and plants it consumes. During the hottest part of the summer, when food is scarce, the ground squirrel retreats to its underground burrow to hibernate.

CHAPTER 3

Living in the Mojave

Indigenous people have been living in and around the Mojave Desert for thousands of years. They knew how to survive during the Mojave's driest, harshest months and learned how to make the most of the few natural resources available to them. European explorers, settlers, and **missionaries** began to explore the Mojave in the 18th century. Today, there are cities and towns within the desert. However, most of the population is concentrated in urban areas that are closer to waterways.

Bullhead City is a large city located on the Colorado River in Mohave County. Spirit Mountain, the highest peak seen from Bullhead City, is a sacred site for the Mojave people. It appears in many Mojave legends as well as legends from other indigenous people.

Fast Fact
The Mojave Desert is situated between the cities of Los Angeles and Las Vegas. The desert is only a one-day drive from 40 million people.

Paleo-Indians

Thousands of years ago, Paleo-Indians lived in and around the Mojave Desert. Paleo-Indians are the earliest known humans in the Americas. These first peoples crossed the Bering Strait from Asia into North America over 10,000 years ago, after the last ice age. Paleo-Indians were nomadic, which means they moved from place to place as the seasons changed. As they traveled, they hunted, fished, and gathered plant foods such as nuts and berries.

Desert Peoples

Indigenous peoples, including the Southern Paiute, the Cahuilla, the Chemehuevi, the Mojave, and the Serrano lived in and around the Mojave Desert after the Paleo-Indians. Some people were farmers, but others were hunter-gatherers. The Chemehuevi, for example, were nomadic hunter-gatherers. They lived on lizards, tortoises, rabbits, seeds, nuts, mesquite beans, and the buds of Joshua trees. They moved with the seasons, traveling to higher elevations in summer and moving to lower elevations in winter. They carried with them everything they needed, including bows, arrows, and knives.

Fast Fact

Native peoples of the Mojave Desert gathered nuts from the Mojave yucca. They roasted the nuts or ate them raw. They extracted fibers from the leaves for weaving baskets, blankets, or ropes.

Over 20,000 ancient Paleo-Indian petroglyphs were found in the Coso Rock Art District.

In 1863, the Chemehuevi lost their traditional territories because the government forced them to move.

15

Beautiful Baskets

Chemehuevi women made complex and beautiful baskets to carry and store water and other items. The baskets were made of desert reeds and grasses that were woven or sewn together. They were then coated with **pitch** so they would not leak. Some baskets could hold 5 gallons (19 L) of water or more. Baskets used for cooking were not placed over an open fire. Instead, heated stones were placed into the baskets to make foods such as soups and stews. The baskets were also used for drying and **winnowing** seeds and nuts, which were harvested from spring to fall.

Mojave men fished in the Colorado River. They caught fish with nets and baskets—and even by hand!

This Mojave woman is carrying water in a specially shaped vessel that balances on her head.

The Mojave

The Mojave people lived in the lowlands along the Colorado River. They were farmers who grew corn, beans, pumpkins, melons, and other foods. Mojave farmers embarked on regular 300-mile (482 km) journeys to the Pacific coast, where they traded pottery and pumpkins for seashells, beads, and other items. The route to the coast stretched the entire width of the Mojave Desert. Today, this trade route is known as the Mojave Road.

Mojave Road

Creeks, streams, springs, and other precious sources of water are important in the Mojave Desert. The Deep Creek Hot Springs are in the northern part of the Mojave on the lower San Bernardino Mountains in California. Deep Creek not only provides desert residents with fresh water, but also contains an abundance of trout which provides food as well.

NOTABLE QUOTE

*"Being **agriculturalists**, the Mohaves had time on their hands and knew where all the springs were… When white men first came through here, they didn't figure their own way. The Indians guided them."*

—Dennis Casebier, Mojave Desert expert

Brittlebush Is Best

Brittlebush is a common plant in the Mojave Desert and in the Sonoran Desert to the south. The stems of the brittlebush secrete a clear **resin**, which indigenous people once used as glue and chewing gum. Other people used the brittlebush twigs as a remedy for toothaches. Grinding the resin and sprinkling it on sores helped to relive pain. Mule deer and bighorn sheep graze on brittlebush. Today, people plant brittlebush near highways to minimize erosion and to restore areas that have been damaged by wildfires.

Fast Fact

Approximately 200 plant species found in the Mojave Desert are endemic plants, which means they grow nowhere else on Earth.

Exploration and Development

One of the first Europeans to travel through the Mojave Desert was a Spanish missionary and explorer named Francisco Garcés. He explored the Mojave, Sonoran, and Colorado deserts, and the Gila and Colorado rivers, from the Gulf of California to the Grand Canyon. Other Mojave Desert explorers include Joaquin Pasqual Nuez, Jedediah Smith, Ewing Young, Kit Carson, and John Fremont. Early European explorers perceived the desert as a barrier to the more hospitable west coast, but the well-traveled trails they used and the discoveries they made about the land are important parts of the Mojave Desert's history. The discovery of gold in the Mojave attracted miners. They established towns that flourished until the gold and other minerals were gone. These towns eventually became **ghost towns**. As the 20th century began, areas with dependable water supplies gave rise to cities. Military bases took over after World War II. A famous general named George S. Patton rolled in tanks and trained troops in the eastern Mojave. In 1994, millions of acres of desert became protected within the Death Valley National Park, the Joshua Tree National Park, and the Mojave National Preserve.

Francisco Garcés

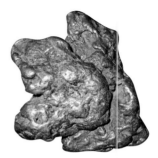

In 1977, prospector Ty Paulsen found the Mojave Nugget. It is believed to be the largest gold nugget found in California.

More than two million people live in the city of Las Vegas.

Desert Cities

Although the Mojave Desert itself is sparsely populated because of the lack of water, it has recently become more urbanized. Many people live on the fringes of the desert or closer to waterways. Las Vegas is the largest city in the Mojave. Large desert cities in California include Lancaster, Palmdale, Victorville, Apple Valley, and Hesperia. Smaller cities in the Mojave include St. George in Utah, and Laughlin in Nevada.

St. George, Utah, is small city with a population close to 75,000. It is known for its trademark red rock cliffs that border the city to the north, as well as the two peaks covered in lava rock in the city's center.

CHAPTER 4

Tourism and Natural Resources

The Mojave Desert is a popular tourist destination. Each year, hundreds of thousands of visitors travel to the national parks and preserves for tours, wildlife viewing, and other activities. Natural resources in the Mojave Desert include silver, gold, and iron. **Borax**, **potash**, and salt are also extracted from certain areas of the desert. Tourism and natural resources contribute to the economic development of the towns and cities within the desert.

Tourists who want to visit Death Valley's Badwater Basin must travel 282 feet (86 m) below sea level. The vast, cracked salt flats covering almost 200 square miles (518 sq km) of the **basin** are made up of sodium chloride, which is better known as salt.

Death Valley National Park

Death Valley National Park is located in the states of California and Nevada, east of the Sierra Nevada Mountains. The northwest corner of the Mojave Desert is within the park. At more than 5,000 square miles (12,950 sq km), it is one of the largest national parks in the United States and has been declared an International **Biosphere** Reserve. Over 800,000 people visited the park in 2011 to witness the wildlife, rugged mountains and canyons, and salt flats in the lowest, hottest, and driest place in North America.

Visitors walk through cracks in the Mosaic Valley's smooth, marble walls.

Tourist Attractions

Each year, hundreds of thousands of tourists visit the national parks and preserves in the Mojave. The Mojave National Preserve is located in the Mojave Desert in San Bernardino Country, California. In 2011, over 500,000 tourists flocked to the preserve to see the Kelso Dunes, Marl Mountains, volcanic formations, forests of Joshua trees, and other natural features. Joshua Tree National Park is located in southeastern California and is named for its forests of Joshua Trees. The park features campsites, hiking trails, and is a popular destination for rock climbers.

These cyclists are riding through Red Rock Canyon in Nevada, which is just 20 miles (32 km) west of Las Vegas.

These large, loose rocks in Joshua Tree National Park are called giant marbles.

Kelso Dunes

Researching and Conserving

The Mojave Desert Heritage & Cultural Association is a non-profit corporation designed to research and conserve the natural and cultural history of the Mojave Desert region. It does so by operating a research center and a library, restoring significant structures, conserving historic open spaces, and producing educational guidebooks and historical publications.

Gold to Ghost

Gold was first discovered in the Mojave Desert in 1848 and the California Gold Rush lasted from 1848–1855. The gold rush brought intensive, but short-lived economic activity to remote towns and villages in the desert. Once the gold and other mineral resources were gone, the towns and villages were abandoned and eventually turned into ghost towns. There are a number of ghost towns in the Mojave Desert such as the Arizona gold-mining town of Oatman, and the California silver-mining town of Calico.

There were over 500 mines in Calico, California. They produced millions of dollars in silver ore over a 12-year span. Today, it is a ghost town.

Solar Gold Rush

The sun is becoming another important natural resource in the Mojave. Gigantic **solar power** plants are being built in the desert. The plants are creating hundreds of construction jobs. When they are completed, the power plants are expected to generate electricity for thousands of homes. One power plant is BrightSource Energy's Ivanpah Solar Electric Generating System, which is located on land near the California-Nevada border. BrightSource uses mirrors to concentrate the sun's energy and turn **turbines** that generate electricity. When complete, Ivanpah will be the largest solar thermal power plant in the world.

Other Resources

Other natural resources in the Mojave include borax, potash, and salt. One of the biggest and richest deposits of borax on the planet is buried deep in the Mojave Desert. The Borax Visitor Center, which was built in 1997, had more than 120,000 visitors at the end of 2010. The visitor center features a museum, mining artifacts, and an observation platform for viewing an open pit mine. Field representatives from the Bureau of Soils and the Geologic Survey discovered potash in the Mojave Desert. They have reason to believe that there are millions of tons of potash in the desert.

The Searles Lake basin is approximately 12 miles (19 km) long and 8.1 miles (13 km) wide. Each year, it yields 1.7 million tons of industrial minerals to the Searles Valley Minerals mining and production company in Overland Park, Kansas.

There are colored rocks on Artist's Palette, which is on the face of the Black Mountains. The colors are caused by the oxidation of different metals.

CHAPTER 5

Desert in Danger

The Mojave Desert may appear to be a harsh environment for the plants and animals that live there, but the desert is actually extremely fragile. The unique plants and animals in the desert are constantly under threat from loss and **degradation** of habitat. Environmental organizations are starting to realize the need to protect the Mojave Desert and the people, plants, and animals living within it.

Fast Fact

The Kelso Dunes in the Mojave National Preserve are home to seven species of endemic insects including the Kelso Dunes Jerusalem cricket and the Kelso Dunes shieldback katydid. These insects live nowhere else on Earth.

Urban Desert

One of the main reasons for habitat loss and degradation in the Mojave Desert is urbanization from large cities nearby. In the last 100 years, Las Vegas has transformed from a desert resort to an urban center. It has a greater metropolitan population of more than two million people and city planners are expecting it to grow by another two million in the next decades. All of these people need food, water, and homes, and roads and highways for transportation. Cities also need spaces for landfills, and the cities of Los Angeles and San Diego are proposing a large landfill in the Mojave Desert region. As land is cleared and built up to make room for these and other necessities, the desert plants and animals lose their habitats.

This picture shows an airplane graveyard in the city of Mojave, California.

Other Threats

Other threats to the desert include agricultural development along the Colorado River, grazing, and the use of off-road vehicles. Experts have determined that the water from the Colorado River consumed for agriculture and by the millions of people in the region now exceeds the total annual flow. State officials are also predicting a ten percent or greater reduction in available water from the river. Livestock grazing damages the small amounts of vegetation in the desert and changes the surfaces of the soil, which can have negative impacts on plants and animals. People who use off-road vehicles in the Mojave cause further damage to the habitats of endangered species and culturally significant archaeological sites.

Desert tortoises and other animals in the Mojave are sometimes crushed by off-road vehicles.

Roads and highways in the Mojave Desert **fragment** the habitats of certain species including the desert tortoise and some species of snakes.

Desert Protection

Governments and environmental organizations are working hard to conserve and protect the Mojave Desert and all the living things that rely on it for their survival. Laws have been passed to protect desert species and much of the Mojave Desert within the Mojave National Preserve, Joshua Tree National Park, Death Valley National Park, and other areas. In fact, the Mojave Desert is one of the most protected eco-regions in the United States! The California Desert Protection League, the California Native Plant Society, the Sierra Club, and The Wilderness Society are all involved in the protection of the Mojave Desert.

Enhance and Protect

The National Parks Conservation Association (www.npca.org) is an organization whose mission is to enhance and protect all of America's national parks, including those within the Mojave, for present and future generations. The Mojave National Preserve received important protection in 1994 when the California Desert Protection Act was passed. However, according to the NPCA, the parks within the Mojave Desert are continually under threat by the growth of southern California and Nevada, environmentally threatening policies, and lack of funding for the protection and management of the park. Scientists and environmentalists must continue to learn about the Mojave Desert so they can protect it for generations to come.

Keep the Sheep!

Desert bighorn sheep are the largest inhabitants of the Mojave Desert. They are named for their large horns, which can weight up to 30 pounds (14 kg). They are often found on steep slopes on or near mountains, on foothills near rocky cliffs, or near water if it is available. They can zigzag up and down cliff faces with great ease, jumping from ledge to ledge over spans as wide as 20 feet (6 m). Desert bighorn sheep have been nearly wiped out by diseases, overhunting, loss of habitat, and habitat fragmentation. In 1959, the Desert Bighorn Council was officially organized to promote the advancement of knowledge about desert bighorn sheep and the long-term welfare of these animals. The council is made up of wildlife biologists, scientists, administrators, managers, and other people interested in the welfare of the desert bighorn sheep.

NOTABLE QUOTE

"The impact of accelerated human and vehicle activity cannot be overstated. Careless mining operations and improper grazing practices have scarred the land. Unplanned construction and road-building have played a destructive game of tic-tac-toe across the desert's face. Excessive and uncontrolled recreational use are undermining the concept of multiple use and removing the desert from the dwindling list of sanctuaries for many rare and endangered species."

—Alan Cranston, former U.S. Senator

COMPARING THE WORLD'S DESERTS

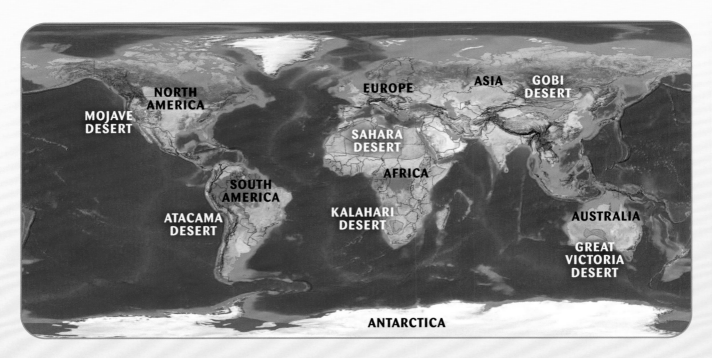

	Continent	Approximate Size	Type of Desert	Annual Precipitation	Natural Resources
Atacama	South America	40,600 square miles (105,154 sq km)	coastal desert	0.04 inches (1 mm)	copper, sodium nitrate, salt, lithium
Gobi	Asia	500,000 square miles (1,294,994 sq km)	cold desert	2–8 inches (5–20 cm)	oil, coal, copper, gold, petroleum, salt
Great Victoria	Australia	161,700 square miles (418,800 sq km)	hot, dry desert	8–10 inches (20–25 cm)	gold, opal, iron ore, copper, coal, oil
Kalahari	Africa	275,000 square miles (712,247 sq km)	semi-arid desert, arid savannah	5–25 inches (13–64 cm)	coal, copper, nickel, and diamonds
Mojave	North America	25,000 square miles (64,750 sq km)	hot, dry desert	2–6 inches (5–15 cm)	copper, gold, solar power
Sahara	Africa	3.5 million square miles (9.1 million sq km)	hot, dry desert	3 inches (8 cm)	coal, oil, natural gas, various minerals

TIMELINE

245–65 million years ago	Earth's tectonic plates collide at fault lines
About 30 million years ago	Earth's crust crack into gigantic blocks; volcanoes form
About 10,000 years ago	Paleo-Indians are living in North America
2000 B.C.E.–C.E. 500	Bow and arrow is introduced into the Mojave region; a relatively moist climate gives way to arid conditions toward the end of this time period
C.E. 500–1200	Large villages are developed; Southern Paiute are living in the Mojave area
1776	Spanish missionary and explorer Francisco Garcés travels through the Mojave Desert
1826–1827	Jedediah Smith crosses the Mojave Desert during a trek to California
1844	John Fremont explores the Mojave
1848	Gold is discovered in the Mojave Desert
1913	Highest reported temperature of 134°F (57°C) in Death Valley
1959	Desert Bighorn Council was officially organized to promote the advancement of knowledge about desert bighorn sheep
1989	Desert tortoise is listed as a threatened species under the Endangered Species Act
1994	Death Valley National Park is established, protecting the northwest corner of the Mojave Desert; Mojave National Preserve is established with the passage of the California Desert Protection Act by U.S. Congress; Joshua Tree National Park is established
2006	United Nations General Assembly declares the year 2006 the International Year of Deserts and Desertification
2011	Over 800,000 people visited Death Valley National Park to view the wildlife, rugged mountains and canyons, and salt flats

GLOSSARY

adapted Changed to fit a new or specific use or situation

aerospace The science that deals with Earth's atmosphere and the space beyond

agriculturalists People who grow food crops and cultivate soil; farmers

basin An area of land drained by a river and its tributaries

biosphere An environment together with the living things that live in it

borax A white, powdery chemical commonly used as a cleaner

burrow A hole in the ground made by an animal for shelter or protection

crust The outer part of Earth

degradation Making or becoming worse

dew Moisture that collects on cool surfaces at night

elevations Heights that are above sea level

erosion The process by which soil and rock are worn away by wind or water

forage To search for food

fragment To break off or split up

friction The rubbing of one thing against another

ghost towns Towns, cities, or villages that have been abandoned

indigenous Living things that are naturally found in a particular region

insulating Preventing the passage of heat into or out of something

landfill An area where trash and garbage is buried between layers of earth

magma Molten rock material within Earth

magma chambers Large underground pools of molten rock beneath Earth's surface

migrating Moving from one country, area, or place to another for feeding or breeding

missionaries People who travel from place to place to try to convert people to a different religion

pitch Resin that comes from trees that bear cones

potash Potassium or a potassium compound

resin Any yellowish or brownish substance that comes from certain trees

sediment Materials, such as stones or sand, deposited by water

solar power Energy derived from the sun and converted into electricity

tectonic plates Gigantic pieces of Earth's crust

toxic Poisonous

turbines Engines with a series of blades

urbanization A process in which cities and other urban areas grow bigger and more developed

winnowing An agricultural method developed by ancient cultures for separating grain from chaff

FIND OUT MORE

BOOKS

Houk, Rose. Mojave Desert (American Deserts Handbook). Western National Parks Association, 2001.

Kalman, Bobbie, and Bishop, Amanda. Nations of the Southwest. Crabtree Publishing Company, 2003.

Rae, Cheri, and McKinney, John. Mojave National Preserve: A Visitor's Guide. The Trailmaster Inc., 2010.

Weeks, John Howard. Mojave Desert (Postcard History). Arcadia Publishing, 2012.

WEBSITES

Mojave Desert
http://mojavedesert.net/

Mojave National Preserve
www.nps.gov/moja/index.htm

DesertUSA
www.desertusa.com/du_mojave.html

Joshua Tree National Park
www.nps.gov/jotr/index.htm

Desert Bighorn Council
http://desertbighorncouncil.org/

INDEX